YOUR LAND AND MY LAND

We Visit

PUERTO RICO

John A. Torres

Mitchell Lane
PUBLISHERS

P.O. Box 196
Hockessin, Delaware 19707

DISCOVER **Puerto Rico** U.S.A.
WHERE THE *Americas* MEET

YOUR LAND
AND
MY LAND

Brazil
Chile
Colombia
Cuba
The Dominican Republic
Mexico
Panama
Peru
Puerto Rico
Venezuela

YOUR LAND AND MY LAND

We Visit

PUERTO RICO

Mitchell Lane

PUBLISHERS

Printing   1   2   3   4   5   6   7   8   9

Library of Congress Cataloging-in-Publication Data
Torres, John Albert.
  We visit Puerto Rico / by John A. Torres.
     p. cm. — (Your land and my land)
  Includes bibliographical references and index.
  ISBN 978-1-58415-892-9 (library bound)
  1. Puerto Rico—Juvenile literature. I. Title.
  F1958.3.T67 2011
  972.95—dc22
                                                              2010011987

PUBLISHER'S NOTE: This story is based on the author's extensive research, which he believes to be accurate. Documentation of his research is on page 61.

  The internet sites referenced herein were active as of the publication date. Due to the fleeting nature of some web sites, we cannot guarantee they will all be active when you are reading this book.

PLB

Contents

Introduction

When people refer to the "Americas," they are referring to what we normally separate into North America, South America, Central America and even Latin America.

While the first three—North, South, and Central—deal with geographic locations, Latin America is distinguished by its language. All the languages spoken in the countries that make up Latin America come from Latin. These include Spanish, Portuguese, and French. These languages, along with Italian, make up the Romance languages.

Nearly 600 million people live in Latin America, which ranges from the southernmost tip of Argentina in South America all the way to the border between Mexico and the United States.

There are more than 20 countries or territories that make up Latin America, including the largest country in South America—Brazil. Others include Haiti, the Dominican Republic, Mexico, Nicaragua, Chile, and Peru.

In this book we will be taking a closer look at a well-known part of Latin America that is not really a country. Not many people realize that Puerto Rico, whose name means "rich port," is actually part of the United States.

Adelpha gelania

FYI Fact:

Butterflies, like the pictured *Adelpha gelania*, have marks on their wings that are thought to be used in attracting mates. This species frequents El Yunque, the rain forest.

Waterfalls, lush vegetation and the sound of tree frogs are prevalent throughout El Yunque.

Co-qui! Co-qui!
Pa-kaw! Pa-kaw!
Can you hear them? Those very loud sounds are made by very tiny tree frogs and colorful parrots perched way up in the trees. If you listen closely, you might be able to hear some wild hogs foraging or some tree monkeys saying hello to each other.

Welcome to Puerto Rico, the only place in the United States where you can visit a real rain forest.

What's that? You didn't know Puerto Rico was part of the United States? Known as a commonwealth territory, the people of Puerto Rico are American citizens and enjoy most of the rights and freedoms that typical Americans have. The people of Puerto Rico vote in American presidential elections but also vote for their own governor, who handles island affairs. This is no different from what happens in each state.

Puerto Rico is an archipelago, meaning it is made up of a main island and several smaller ones. It is in the northeastern Caribbean Sea, west of the Virgin Islands and east of the island of Hispaniola, which is home to Haiti and the Dominican Republic. It is about 1,000 miles (1,600 km) southeast of Miami, Florida.

You might be surprised to know that even though the U.S. has hundreds of national parks and forests, its only tropical rain forest is on the small island of Puerto Rico. Called El Yunque, the tropical rain forest is located on the eastern half of the island and boasts thousands of native plants, including 150 fern species and 240 tree species. Some of the trees and some of the small animals that live there cannot be found anyplace else on the planet.

In fact, those lucky enough to visit can hear the nonstop serenade of song coming from the trees and thick brush: *Co-qui! Co-qui!* But they would be hard pressed to pinpoint the source of the beautiful singsong. Tiny Puerto Rican tree frogs, known as coquis, call out to each other all night long. They often cling to the underside of leaves. Their song is interrupted only when lightning flashes or the rare Puerto Rican parrot creates a ruckus with its caw.

Little tree frogs known as coquis sing throughout the night and can be heard just about anywhere on the island where there is vegetation.

Many tropical islands in the Caribbean are home to exotic and colorful birds like the parrot. Puerto Rico is no exception.

The thunder that occurs during the intense lightning storms sound like a hammer smashing down onto an anvil. The Spanish word for anvil is *yunque*. Those storms, as well as the steady rainfall that produces up to 240 inches of rain a year, give the 28,000-acre park its name.

While the people of Puerto Rico take great pride in El Yunque, the island offers so much more. Cruise ships and tourists from around the world vacation there. Popular for its historical sites as well as for its native beauty, the country boasts hiking trails and salsa dancing, stargazing and fine art.

FYI Fact:

To express their nationality, Puerto Ricans say, "*Soy de aquí como el coquí*" (I'm as Puerto Rican as a coquí).

In truth, Puerto Rico is a unique destination because of the native Taíno Indian, European, American, and African influences on the culture. The people of Puerto Rico like to be referred to as *boricua*, a Taíno word for someone born and raised on the island.

In the early 1500s, Spanish invaders, accompanied by enslaved people from Africa, conquered the island's original inhabitants, the Taíno Indians. The United States claimed the island after defeating Spain in a war in 1898.

Like many Caribbean islands, Puerto Rico's main source of income is through agriculture; its main crops are sugarcane and coffee. Industry, mainly in the field of manufacturing, is a close second behind agriculture. Tourism is also a moneymaker for the island.

Puerto Ricans use U.S. currency on the island and follow the same type of school and educational systems as those in the United States. But the American influence can be seen no more clearly than on the baseball field. Puerto Ricans love baseball.

The island has produced many famous baseball players, including the great Roberto Clemente and Orlando Cepeda. Later baseball stars from Puerto Rico include Carlos Beltran, Benjie Molina, Alex Rios, and Carlos Delgado.

Puerto Ricans have also made their mark on American pop culture in the music and movie industries. Some notables include singer Marc Anthony, actress Rosario Dawson, Academy Award–winning actor Benicio del Toro, actor and comedian John Leguizamo, and many others.

Puerto Rican food has risen in popularity in the United States as more people are expanding their tastes to include more ethnic dishes. A traditional Puerto Rican dish is arroz con pollo, or chicken and rice.

FYI Fact:

A Taíno legend says that the good spirit "Yuquiyu" protected the Taínos from his mountaintop throne located in the El Yunque rain forest.

This European drawing of a Taíno family shows the respect and reliance the culture had for nature and wildlife.

WHERE IN THE WORLD IS PUERTO RICO?

ATLANTIC OCEAN

Arecibo · San Juan
Aguadilla · · Carolina
Bayamon · Trujillo Alto · Fajardo US UK
Utuado · Guaynabo · Isla de Culebra St Thomas
Mayaguez · Caguas · Charlotte Amalie St John
+ Cerro de Punta
4390 · Cayey Humacao
Yauco · Ponce · Isla de Vieques
Guayama
Isla Mona

CARIBBEAN SEA

Christiansted
St Croix

PUERTO RICO

AND THE

U.S. VIRGIN ISLANDS

MILES
0   10   20   30   40   50

Where in the World

The small islands off Puerto Rico's east coast are part of the commonwealth as well. They are Culebra Island and Vieques island.

With lush forests, white sand beaches, historic forts, breathtaking mountains, infectious musical rhythms, and delicious foods, it's no wonder that Puerto Rico is known as La Isla del Encanto, which means "The Island of Enchantment."

PUERTO RICO
FACTS AT A GLANCE

Hibiscus

Full name: The Commonwealth of Puerto Rico
Languages: Spanish, English
Population: 3,966,213 (July 2009 est.)
Total area: 3,508 square miles (9,104 square kilometers)
Land area: 3,435 square miles (8,959 square kilometers)
Capital: San Juan
Ethnic makeup: White (Spanish origin) 76.2%, black 6.9%, Asian 0.3%, mixed 4.4%, other 12%
Religion: Roman Catholic 85%, Protestant and other 15%
Climate: Tropical
Average temperature: January: 76°F, 24.4°C ; August: 82°F, 27.7°C
Average annual rainfall: 53 in (135 cm)
Highest point: Cerro Punta—4,389 ft (1,338 m)
Longest river: Grande de Arecibo—40 miles (64 km)
Commonwealth flower: Puerto Rican hibiscus
Commonwealth bird: Stripe-headed tanager
Flag:

Stripe-headed tanager

The Puerto Rican flag was officially adopted on July 25, 1952. The three sides of its blue, equilateral triangle represent the three branches of Puerto Rico's Republican government (executive, legislative, and judicial branches). The white, five-pointed star stands for the Commonwealth of Puerto Rico. The 3 red stripes stand for the blood that supports the government. The 2 white stripes stand for human rights and individual freedom. The Puerto Rican flag is always flown in the company of the United States flag.

*Sources: CIA World Factbook: Puerto Rico; http://www.topuertorico.org/reference/flag.shtml

Beautiful monuments are the centerpiece of many plazas or town squares. A statue of Christopher Columbus stands in Plaza de Colón in Old San Juan.

A Brief History

On November 14, 1493, Christopher Columbus landed on the island of Puerto Rico with 17 ships and about 1,500 men. He named the island San Juan Bautista, which means "St. John the Baptist." To this day, San Juan remains the capital of Puerto Rico. The Spaniards established a home base, called Caparra, which was run by Juan Ponce de León, an explorer who served under Columbus. A year later, Ponce de León figured it made more sense to move the city closer to a suitable port so that they could readily receive supplies. He named the settlement Puerto Rico. Twenty-five years later, the two names were switched—the port became San Juan, and the island, Puerto Rico.

A walk around San Juan reveals Puerto Rico's colonial past. Still standing in historic Old San Juan is a beautiful white building known as La Casa Blanca (the White House). Built in 1521, it was Ponce de León's home. It is now the National Historic Monument, a museum with exhibits from the sixteenth, seventeenth, and eighteenth centuries, including many Taíno Indian artifacts.

There are not many historical documents for Puerto Rico from before Columbus arrived. However, there are plenty of archaeological clues that can teach us something about what kind of people lived on the island. Evidence suggests that several tribes took turns inhabiting the island thousands of years before Columbus was even born.

The Ortoiroid people are believed to have settled on the island between 3000 and 2000 BCE. These Indians probably traveled from regions in South America to inhabit many Caribbean islands, especially the area known as the West Indies. Remains from archaeological digs suggest these people were fishermen and relied on the ocean for their food.

Over the years, the Ortoiroid people were replaced by the Saladoid people, who came from around the same region as the Ortoiroid people. However, while the Ortoiroid people were fishermen, the Saladoid people were farmers. They also are credited with bringing pottery to this region. Perhaps they would store the food they grew in the decorated red pots they made.

They apparently lived there peacefully, but were eventually replaced by another peace-loving people known as the Arawaks. The term *Arawak* refers to a number of different Indian tribes that shared the Arawak language. One of the tribes that evolved from the Arawak, the Taíno Indians, would dominate Puerto Rico for many years.

The Taíno culture was a combination of all the cultures that came before them. They hunted and fished like the Ortoiroids, grew large farms like the Saladoids, and gathered roots like the Arawaks. The culture was so advanced that the people—maybe for the first time in this region—had leisure time. They built ball fields and developed games with very specific rules. They also began practicing religion. Their elaborate set of beliefs included the worship of several gods and goddesses.

A little more than an hour's drive from San Juan is the town of Jayuya, in the center of the island. It is believed that the Taínos lived in the area of Jayuya, and the town continues to celebrate the culture. In the town is the truly unique Cemi Museum. It looks like a giant stone carving of one of the Taíno gods. While the building is spectacular, inside there are many Taíno treasures, including tools, and carvings.

The Taínos believed that it was important to keep their gods happy because they would protect them from disasters such as hurricanes, floods, bad crops, and disease. But they could not protect them from the Spaniards.

While the Spaniards were impressed with how the Taínos lived, their ultimate goal was to strip the island of its riches and any gold that may be there. The Spaniards promised to protect the Taínos, but in reality they enslaved them. The Taínos eventually revolted and tried to fight the Spaniards. They were no match for the Spanish army, with their modern weapons and tactics. With casualties from warfare and from the

Cemi Museum in Jayuya

European diseases to which the Taínos had no immunity, the Taíno civilization came to an end.

The Spanish ruled the island for decades, but they had to fight to keep it. They withstood many attacks from the French and the English. Finally, in the late 1590s, the English arrived with a large fleet of ships filled with men. They set fire to San Juan and took the island.

Their triumph did not last long. Many of the Englishmen became ill, and within a few months they abandoned what they had gained. The Spaniards retook the island and rebuilt San Juan.

Under Spanish rule the island became poorer and poorer, because the Spaniards were removing the natural resources such as gold and other valuable commodities. The people, now a mixture of Spanish settlers, Taíno Indians, and some African slaves, had developed an identity of their own and wanted independence from Spain.

In 1868, organized protests targeted the Spanish rulers. Puerto Rican leaders reached out to U.S. President William McKinley for help. They knew the United States wanted to end the Spanish influence in the Caribbean. In April 1898, the Spanish-American War began.

In August of that year, U.S. forces defeated the Spaniards and took control of Cuba, Puerto Rico, and various islands in the western Pacific Ocean. The U.S. has governed the Puerto Rico ever since.

Water sports are very popular in Puerto Rico. Surfers take advantage of the waves crashing on Culebra Island.

Chapter 3

The Land and Animals

Puerto Rico's location between the Caribbean Sea and the North Atlantic Ocean make it an important piece of land—which is why Spain, France, Great Britain, and the United States were so interested in the island. Strategically, a military based there would have access to the United States and other Caribbean islands. Besides its strategic importance, Puerto Rico lies along many trade routes through the Caribbean.

Puerto Rico is an archipelago, which means it is made up of several islands. The main island, Puerto Rico, is not very big. In fact, it is only 110 miles (180 kilometers) long and 40 miles (65 kilometers) wide. In addition to the main island, the Commonwealth of Puerto Rico includes the islands of Vieques, Culebra, Mona, Desecheo, and Caja de Muertos, as well as many even smaller islands. People live on the main island, Vieques, and Culebra year-round; many of the other islands are strictly nature preserves.

Many tourists decide to end their busy vacations with a few days on the islands. Culebra Island, for example, is advertised as a place to go to when you want to do nothing! Tourists can lounge on Culebra's gorgeous beaches, such as Flamenco Beach, or they can go snorkeling at the nearby coral reefs. In Bioluminescent Bay off Vieques, people can swim at night for a chance to glow in the dark. Also known as Mosquito Bay, this lagoon is filled with millions of single-celled organisms that flash a blue light when they are agitated. Their light is so bright, you can actually read a book by it! You can see fish swim along

Flamenco Beach on Culebra Island. The word *Culebra* means "snake." The tiny island is actually another archipelago. It includes the main island of Culebra plus 23 smaller islands.

as the organisms light the way. Some people say that swimming in the water feels like floating through the stars.

The main island of Puerto Rico has three distinct geographic regions: the mountainous region, the coastal plains, and the northern karst. A karst is an area dotted with sinkholes and riddled with underground streams.

Puerto Rico's mountains lie mainly in the center of the island and consist of the following ranges: La Cordillera Central, La Sierra de

Cayey, La Sierra de Luquillo, and La Sierra Bermeja. The highest point is Cerro Punta, which is 4,389 feet (1,338 meters) high. This mountain is located in La Cordillera Central. While it is not even half as high as Mount Everest, it is still an impressive sight.

Because of the mountain ranges in the center of the island, Puerto Rico also has no real long rivers. The longest river is the Grande de Arecibo, which flows to the northern coast. Some of the island's other rivers include La Plata, Cibuco, Loíza, Bayamón, and Grande de Añasco.

The karst area is located in the northern interior mountainous part of the island. Huge areas of limestone rock dissolved over thousands and thousands of years to create the underwater streams and unique land formations there. The karst also has many plateaus, some with elevations of nearly 1,000 feet. Near the interior of the karst region are countless hills, caves, and sinkholes. Some of these caves have yet to be fully explored. The underground streams are especially mysterious. For example, there is one river—Rio de Camuy—that flows over this area and then suddenly disappears underground. The river resurfaces several miles down a hill. It is the third largest underwater river in the United States.

Rio Camuy Cave Park near Arecibo is definitely worth the 70-minute car trip from San Juan. The 268-acre park holds more than 200 caves that were carved out by the Camuy River more than a million years ago. Follow the paved paths—you can even wear sandals—down more than 200 feet to the wonderful caves. The park's largest cave—Cueva Clara—is 695 feet (212 meters) long.

For future geologists, the caves contain many examples of crystallized formations known as stalactites and stalagmites. One of the caverns, Clara de Empalme Cave, is 180 feet (55 meters) high. Throughout the caves and caverns live millions of bats. You can also search the water in these caves for a rare species of blind fish.

Nearby is the Arecibo Observatory, which is home to the world's largest single-dish radio telescope. More than 100,000 people visit the observatory each year. About 200 scientists and numerous students use the observatory every year for researching the planet, atmosphere, and space.

The coastal plains are made up of some of the world's most beautiful beaches. These areas of famous white sand beaches are where the majority of tourists go.

Mona Island has been called the "Galápagos of Puerto Rico" for its giant iguanas and sea turtles. For nature lovers who want to see a wide variety of wildlife in one day, try a trip to the Las Cabezas de San Juan Nature Reserve. There you can experience seven different ecosystems, including forestland, mangroves, lagoons, beaches, cliffs,

A sea turtle swims off the coast of Puerto Rico. The waters around the island are teeming with life.

and offshore coral reefs.

Because Puerto Rico is in the tropics, it is usually hot and humid there. The average temperature is about 80 degrees Fahrenheit (26°C),

Arecibo Observatory

and there is very little change throughout the year. The only place on the island that has cooler temperatures is in the mountain regions. Like other countries with tropical climates, Puerto Rico has two seasons: the dry season and the wet season.

The dry season typically runs from the end of October through May, and the wet season from June to November. This is very similar to the wet and dry seasons in Florida as well. Also similar to Florida, people in Puerto Rico have to be wary of hurricanes between June and November. Many hurricanes have caused severe damage and death on the island.

Believe it or not, Puerto Rico has about 15 lakes or reservoirs, but none of them are natural. People flooded certain areas in order to collect the water in basins. This was done for irrigation purposes. Many of the island's short rivers and streams have been dammed to produce hydroelectric power.

Puerto Rico does not have many large animals. There are some monkeys on the island that were brought in or escaped, and plenty of iguanas and lizards roaming free. One animal you might be surprised to find there is the mongoose. This animal is typically found in Asia and naturally hunts smaller rodents and snakes. In the nineteenth century, sugarcane farmers imported the mongoose to control the rat

Cueva Clara in Rio Camuy Cave Park. Puerto Rico's landscape offers something for everyone. Besides caves, there are rain forests, mountains, and beaches.

populations that were eating their crops. The rats were also not native to Puerto Rico—they arrived as stowaways on the ships from Spain.

The experiment failed. The mongoose population did not eat the rats. Instead they destroyed some of the island's native bird populations.

Puerto Rico's tropical climate, rainfall amounts, and access to sunshine create the perfect recipe for an incredibly diverse flora, or types of plant life. Palm trees sway on the beaches; mahogany trees, ferns, and orchids thrive in the rain forest; and cactus and bunch grass dot the dry southwest.

After a day chasing lizards or swimming at the beach, kids will want to make sure they get a chance to visit the Heladería de Lares, or the Lares Ice Cream Parlor. Do you think some American ice cream parlors have lots of flavors? Heladería de Lares has more than 1,000 flavors, including corn, cod, and chicken.

A thunderstorm looms off the island's coast. Hot temperatures during the summer months make Puerto Rico prone to thunderstorms and even hurricanes.

Generally speaking, Puerto Ricans are friendly people who love being in the company of others. Men and women dress in light clothing to help stay cool.

The People

What started out as a small island inhabited by the Taíno Indians has become a modern cosmopolitan territory with a unique blend of people. The capital city of San Juan is a bustling business center as well as a historical living museum and tourist resort center. There are universities and cultural centers. But just miles away in the mountain villages, the atmosphere and culture seem very different.

How did this blend of people come about?

Many of the Spanish soldiers who were stationed on the island married Taíno women and had children. As commerce on the island grew and the Spanish stronghold became more established, there was a need for cheap or free labor to help maintain the farms and build more roads. For these tasks, the Spanish enslaved people from Africa.

Modern Puerto Rico is a mixture of European Spaniards, Taíno Indians, and Africans. But there are other influences as well. Chinese immigrants began arriving in waves in the late nineteenth century and then again in the 1950s, when they were fleeing Fidel Castro's communist Cuba. Some businesses and places have Chinese names, including a valley in the town of Maunabo, which is called Quebrada los Chinos or the Chinese Stream.

German, French, Irish, Lebanese, and Italian immigrants have also helped shape the Puerto Rican identity. Many of these European people settled in Puerto Rico in the 1800s after Spain issued the Royal Decree of Graces in 1815, which encouraged Spaniards and other Europeans to come by granting them land there. Spain believed this tactic would help ensure the island remained a Catholic nation.

The Spaniards made sure to build plenty of churches where people could practice their faith. In fact, the first Catholic diocese in the colony was built in San Juan in 1511. (A diocese oversees all the Catholic

San Juan is a charming city that combines modern business, tourism, and history. Almost one third of the population of Puerto Rico lives in the area of San Juan, Bayamon, and Carolina.

San Blas de Illescas

churches in a particular area.) The churches provided the center of social activity for a town, so they were normally built with a large plaza around them for people to gather. Just about every town or city on the island has a Catholic church.

While Old San Juan has its share of cathedrals and churches, you can also find historical religious buildings in many other parts of Puerto Rico. For example, in the city of Coamo, you'll be able to visit a huge whitewashed church known as San Blas de Illescas. Built in 1661, it was renovated in 1784. The building overlooks Coamo's town plaza.

Puerto Rico remains mainly Catholic, though other religions are practiced there as well. For example, during the 1950s there was a large influx of Jewish businessmen who moved to the island with their families. Now Puerto Rico has the largest Jewish population of any island in the Caribbean. There are also a few Muslim communities, though their numbers make up less than one percent of the nearly four million people who live there.

Even though Puerto Rico is a territory of the United States, Spanish remains the primary language. However, English is also listed as an official language, and it is taught as a second language in public schools.

Ray Barretto (1929–2006) was called the godfather of Latin jazz and salsa music. Today, no party or festival in Puerto Rico is complete without the pulsing rhythms of salsa and the sight of people dancing.

It's difficult to decide where to start when taking a look at Puerto Rican culture. Do we start with the rich foods like rice and beans with roasted bananas and pork? Do we start with the pulsing salsa music and island dances? Do we start with famous Puerto Rican literature like El Gibaro (or El Jibaro), which mixes poetry and prose? Or with the architecture, which boasts many styles, including neo-classical, Baroque, and even Gothic?

Perhaps the most obvious place to start is in San Juan—with the architecture. Of note are the city's winding, narrow cobblestone streets. They are are narrow because they were built when people traveled by horse and not by car. Buildings sporting red-tile roofs are perfect examples of colonial Spanish architecture. These beautiful homes often have heavy wooden doors that lead to open-air courtyards. They are similar to the types of buildings found in the south of Spain. What makes them typically Puerto Rican is this: The streets and the walls around the city are made of sand and seashells!

Spain was worried that other navies or even pirates would try to attack San Juan, so huge sandstone walls were built around the city, and a massive fortress, El Morro, was constructed. The fort, standing on the banks of San Juan Bay, has been there for more than 400 years.

A nearby smaller fort, La Fortaleza, built in 1533, was erected to protect the people of San Juan from other native Caribbean peoples. It is still in use today as the home for the governor of Puerto Rico.

Keep an eye out for a hotel known as El Convento. This 350-year-old building used be a convent for Carmelite nuns of the Catholic Church. It has had many uses over the years, but in the 1990s it was converted to a small luxury hotel. It is within walking distance of many of the city's historical sites and architectural wonders.

What would a trip to Puerto Rico be without sampling some of the island's cuisine? In Old San Juan, numerous street vendors sell all types of typical Puerto Rican food, including *bacalaitos*, which are fried codfish fritters and are as popular as hotdogs are in the states. They also offer refreshment from the high temperatures with *piragua,* which is similar to a snow cone. *Piragua* stands, run by *piragüeros*, have huge blocks of ice. The *piragüeros* shave the ice into a paper cup and then pour the flavored syrup of your choice over them. The stands, or carts, are painted very brightly so that kids can spot them from afar. There are also Puerto Rican soft drinks for kids called *malta*—which is wheat soda. It has the same ingredients as beer, but since it has not gone through the process of fermentation, it contains no alcohol.

Of course Puerto Rican cuisine goes way beyond street vendors selling fried fish. Not surprisingly, the food combines the influences that make up the Puerto Rican people: Spanish, Taíno Indian, and African.

The Taíno Indians cooked with items found on or grown on the island, such as coriander, papaya and plantains. The Spaniards introduced beef, pork, rice, and wheat. The Africans introduced okra and many root-based vegetables such as taro. The food in Puerto Rico today is a spicy blend of all three. Many popular foods include meat pies, chicken with rice, and *pasteles*—ground plantains stuffed with meat and vegetables.

Desserts feature just about anything that can go with coconut, such as rice puddings and custards like flan—a caramel-based pudding. Meals are typically topped off with strong Puerto Rican coffee, grown on the island's mountain ranges.

Two distinct types of music define Puerto Rico: jibaro and salsa. You are more likely to hear jibaro, a type of folk music, in small towns or mountain villages, but street singers in San Juan may be playing jibaro on their guitars as well. These simple songs are usually romantic ballads or funny stories and are played on a variety of string instruments, including the guitar. The word *salsa* means "sauce." Some say the music was named salsa because it is the sauce that gets a party started.

Salsa music was actually started by Puerto Ricans living in New York City shortly after the end of World War II. The rhythms are very African sounding, with pounding drums and intricate drumming sequences. The popularity of salsa music spread back to Puerto Rico, where some of the world's top salsa singers have emerged. The music has a big band jazz feel as well as African and Caribbean rhthyms.

Puerto Ricans have made their mark in literature as well. Perhaps the first really well-known piece of writing is an 1849 piece by Manuel Alonso Pacheco called *El Jibaro*.

The nineteenth century also produced very talented Puerto Rican poets. Lola Rodriguez de Tió, José Gautier Benítez, and José Gualberto Padilla all thrived as romantic and lyrical poets who were able to express their love of their island home through their beautiful words.

Puerto Ricans also love to compete in sports. Baseball is the most popular sport on the island, and there is a professional league that boasts numerous teams. Many of their players also play Major League Baseball.

Just about every major city on the island has a professional baseball team and stadium. Sometimes, if you make it out to a ballgame, you'll be lucky enough to catch a rising superstar or even an established Major League Baseball player who is recovering from an injury.

The island has also produced many good boxers, such as world champion Felix Trinidad. Basketball and soccer have also become popular in Puerto Rico, but neither rivals the love Puerto Ricans have for baseball.

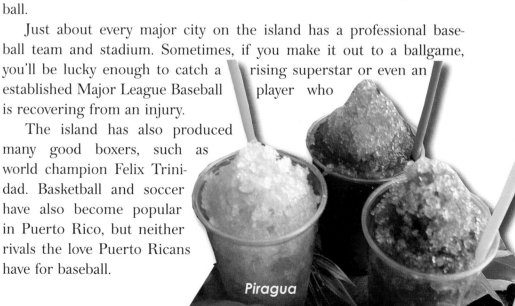

Piragua

This vintage photo shows a man working in a sugarcane field in the 1930s. Puerto Rico's economy used to rely mainly on the sugarcane harvest.

Chapter 6

Economy and Commerce

For many years the economy of Puerto Rico could be summed up in one word: sugar. The island climate is perfect for growing sugarcane, and as the popularity of the alcoholic drink rum grew, so did the need for more sugar.

Sugarcane originated in Asia. It was introduced in Europe way before Christopher Columbus decided to plant some in the Caribbean in 1493. The first sugarcane fields were planted in the Dominican Republic in 1501. There is no exact date for the introduction of sugarcane to Puerto Rico, but most believe that Juan Ponce de León commissioned the first fields, and the first processing plant was built in 1523. The first versions of sugarcane were planted so that people could chew on the sweet stalks.

Sugar was the main crop and the main source of income for Puerto Rico for hundreds of years. As other countries began exporting sugar, the factories and farms in Puerto Rico began to shut down.

Poverty began to spread. To improve economic conditions on the island, President Franklin D. Roosevelt organized the Puerto Rican Reconstruction Administration, which looked at different ways to help the island. He initiated what became known as Operation Bootstrap. This gave employers and investors tax breaks if they switched from farming to manufacturing or other industries.

The move to industry and manufacturing was wise and necessary. Puerto Rico lacks valuable natural resources like copper, gold, or oil, so the island has to look elsewhere for sources of income.

The tax breaks worked, as many companies—especially the ones that make medicines and chemicals—moved their operations to Puerto Rico. They provided new employment opportunities for the people of the island. For example, even though Puerto Rico is not among the world's leaders in making clothes, more than 30,000 people on the island work in the clothing manufacturing business.

The idea was to focus on creating items to be exported to—or sold to—the people of the United States. It worked well in general, and Puerto Rico is known to have one of the best economies in the Caribbean, but there is also a problem.

Since the main market for these goods is the American public, then the health of the Puerto Rican economy relies heavily on the American one. When there is a recession or a slowdown in the U.S. economy, then Puerto Rico's economy suffers as well.

Luckily, when manufacturing companies are not doing well, there is another way for the island to generate money: tourism.

People are drawn from all over the world to the white sand beaches and five-star hotels that make the tropical island a popular destination for travelers. Many of them arrive on cruise ships. There are also seven airports on the island. San Juan is populated with gorgeous hotels and resorts, many of them with breathtaking ocean views.

To accommodate the approximately 5 million tourists that visit the island every year, the construction industry is normally busy as well. There is steady need for new hotels and renovations for older ones. When the Puerto Rico Convention Center was built, it was the largest convention center in the Caribbean, able to cater to 10,000 people at a time.

Tourism brings about $2 billion to the island every year and the industry employs thousands of people, from managers to maids. In fact, more than 60,000 people are employed because of the tourism industry.

A very small sector of the island still relies on agriculture. Instead of sugarcane, cattle and chickens are raised. Very few farmers still rely on growing crops. Those who do grow coffee, pineapples, plantains, and bananas.

Puerto Rico's climate makes it suitable for growing many different crops, including the banana trees on this plantation.

As long as the island of Puerto Rico remains a commonwealth—property of the United States—it will receive federal aid. For example, in 2006, there was a major financial breakdown in Puerto Rico, and its government was running out of cash. Things got so bad that for a short time all the government workers—including schoolteachers—were sent home because there was no money to pay them. The crisis and money shortage were fixed when the U.S. government approved a small increase to the island's sales tax.

A painting of Luis Muñoz Marín, the first governor of Puerto Rico. He is remembered as the Father of modern Puerto Rico.

Politics and Government

The Commonwealth of Puerto Rico has never really been an independent nation. The only time the island freely governed itself was before Spanish colonial rule, when the Taíno Indians were established on the island.

But what exactly is a commonwealth? Is Puerto Rico a colony of the United States? Who is in charge there?

What's important to know is that people in Puerto Rico are in the United States. If you travel there from any other part of the United States, you don't need a passport. Still, once you get off the plane or cruise ship in Puerto Rico, it definitely feels as if you are in a foreign country.

Ownership of the island was transferred from Spain to the U.S. in 1898, after the Spanish-American War. But while the Spaniards allowed the people of Puerto Rico much say in running their own affairs, the U.S. government did things differently. Even though the U.S. president appointed a governor to oversee the island, the U.S. Congress wrote and approved a law called the Foraker Act of 1900. This law gave the Puerto Rican people the right to form a House of Representatives—similar to the one already in Washington, D.C. The people could then vote for their local leaders.

In 1917, another law was enacted that drew Puerto Rico and the U.S. even closer. The Jones-Shafroth Act made all Puerto Ricans citizens of the U.S. This was a big deal. It gave the people basically the same rights as any other American. It is very rare for a powerful country like the United States to grant citizenship. Once Puerto Ricans were free to move from the island to the U.S. mainland, many moved permanently to the states, looking for better jobs or a better way of life.

The Jones-Shafroth Act also allowed the people of Puerto Rico to form a Senate. Now the people were able to elect members to their House of Representatives and to their Senate. The government of Puerto Rico became a mini Republic, a mirror image of the U.S. government, with an executive, legislative, and judicial branch.

Because Puerto Ricans were granted citizenship, the U.S. government could draft them into the armed forces and send them to war. The author's grandfather, Juan Calderon, was drafted from his Puerto Rican home to serve in the U.S. Army during World War I.

This "partnership" between the United States and Puerto Rico did not always go smoothly. For example, there were some violent protests in the 1930s by people who wanted more from the United States, especially in the form of aid after natural disasters such as hurricanes.

In 1946, President Harry S. Truman appointed the first Puerto Rican–born governor of the island, Jesús T. Piñero. The island was still considered a "non-incorporated territory." This is the same status that territories such as Oklahoma and New Mexico had before becoming states. Only a year after Piñero was appointed, the U.S. Congress passed a law allowing Puerto Ricans to vote for their governor.

History was made on November 2, 1948, when Luis Muñoz Marín, who was president of the Senate, became the first democratically elected leader of Puerto Rico. Marín was a well-educated man who wrote books of poetry, worked as a journalist, and was a champion for the working class. While moving his way up the political ranks, he seemed to be in favor of establishing the independent country of Puerto Rico. But Marín did not like the aggressive and sometimes radical thinking by those who wanted independence. He wanted to do what was best for the people, and eventually he thought that what was best was to maintain the existing close relationship to the United States.

In 1950, the United States allowed Puerto Ricans to establish and write their own constitution, one that established the island as a commonwealth of the United States. In a commonwealth, everyone is equal, and they work for the common good of everyone involved.

Marín, whom *Time* magazine voted as one of the most influential politicians of the twentieth century, governed Puerto Rico from 1949 to 1964. There were many people who want-

Capitol Building in Puerto Rico

ed him to continue to be governor, but he agreed with a small group of protesters who felt that governors should be in office for only two four-year terms. He told his saddened supporters, "I am not your strength. . . . You are your own strength."

While the U.S. has two major political parties, the people of Puerto Rico have three. One party favors independence, another party favors statehood, and a third party prefers to keep the commonwealth status.

Puerto Rico remains a commonwealth of the U.S., though there has been a growing movement over the years to make Puerto Rico the fifty-first state. In 1967, 1993, and 1998, the people could choose whether they preferred independence, statehood, or the current commonwealth status. All three times, the people voted to keep things as they were.

The U.S. government has never said that it would yield to the outcome of the votes, but it wanted to see how the people felt.

According to *People* magazine, Jennifer Lopez, New York–born daughter of Puerto Rican parents, is the most influential Hispanic entertainer of today. She is an accomplished singer, actress, and dancer.

Chapter 8

Famous People

You've seen the beaches, visited the historic sites, tried your hand at reading some classic Puerto Rican literature, and sampled the food. Now let's learn a little bit about some of the famous people who have come from this land.

No section about famous Puerto Ricans is complete without a closer look at the first democratically elected governor of the island, Luis Muñoz Marín.

Luis Muñoz Marín

Marín was born in 1898, the same year that Spain lost control of the island to the United States. An educated man, Marín spent much of his youth traveling and going to schools in the United States, including Georgetown University in Washington, D.C. His family moved to New York, and Marín found success as a poet and a journalist.

But Marín was moved by the poverty of his homeland and longed to return there to help the people. In 1932 he officially

PUERTO RICO'S
GOVERNOR MUÑOZ MARIN

entered the world of politics and was elected Senator. He worked his way up to the presidency of the Senate, and then in 1948 was elected the governor of the island.

He served in office for sixteen years, and in 1963 was awarded the Presidential Medal of Freedom. Even after he stepped down as governor, Marín stayed active in the Puerto Rican Senate until 1970.

He spent the twilight of his life traveling, before returning to Puerto Rico, his health failing. He died in 1980 and is remembered as "the father of modern Puerto Rico."

Rita Moreno

World-class actress and singer Rita Moreno was born in Puerto Rico in 1931 in the town of Humacao. She is known for many famous roles that she brought to life, including Anita in *West Side Story*, and became the first woman to win the four biggest awards in show business. She won an Academy Award for her role as Anita (1961), a Tony Award for her theater work (1975), an Emmy Award for outstanding television work (1977), and a Grammy for her singing (1972). She is one of only 10 performers to have won all four awards.

Her family moved to New York City when she was only five years old. A few years later, wanting a career in show business, Moreno started to do voiceover work for American films dubbed into Spanish.

Moreno has remained busy acting in television shows and movies. She has appeared on the hit television shows *Ugly Betty*, *Law and Order*, and *The George Lopez Show*.

Roberto Clemente

Roberto Clemente is one of Puerto Rico's truest heroes. While his skills as a Major League Baseball player were good enough to earn him a spot in the baseball Hall of Fame, it was Clemente's spirit of helping others that makes him a legend.

Clemente was born in 1934 in a town called Carolina. He was the youngest of seven children. From an early age it was clear that Clemente was going to be a great baseball player. He had a strong throwing arm, was a fast runner, could hit for power and average, and was a great fielder. While he was playing for a Puerto Rican team, scouts from the Brooklyn Dodgers noticed him. They signed him to a contract, but it was mainly to keep him from being signed by the New York Giants. A few years later, the Pittsburgh Pirates signed him, and that's where he stayed.

Over the course of a stellar career, Clemente won many awards and helped his team win the World Series. He was voted the Most Valuable Player one year and finished his career with 3,000 hits. His other passion was helping others. He planned to build a huge sports complex for children in his native land.

On December 31, 1972, Clemente boarded a plane filled with supplies he had helped collect to assist the people of the country of Nicaragua, which had suffered from a massive earthquake. The plane crashed shortly after takeoff, and Clemente was killed.

He became a national hero.

Julia de Burgos

Another famous Puerto Rican who died young was Julia de Burgos, a teacher, writer, and poet. Like Clemente, she was born in Carolina. She is considered by many to have been one of the twentieth century's most influential poets.

She graduated from the University of Puerto Rico with a teaching degree, then dedicated her time to teaching elementary school children and working for the independence movement. But it was her love of literature that shaped who she was.

She wrote many famous poems, including "Río Grande de Loíza," which is a breathtaking look at the emotions Burgos had for this Puerto Rican river. In the poem, she says the river may have been formed by tears, perhaps her own.

She published several books of poetry before moving to New York City. She died there of pneumonia at the age of thirty-nine.

José Feliciano

José Feliciano has been impressing music lovers for decades with his melodic voice and incredible guitar playing. He was born blind in 1945 in the town of Lares. His family moved to Spanish Harlem in New York City when he was five years old, and a year later he taught himself how to play a concertina—which is like a small accordion—just by listening to records. By the time he was eight years old, Feliciano was performing in his school for his classmates.

After he mastered the concertina, Feliciano taught himself how to play the guitar, again using only records and practicing fourteen hours a day. He has won numerous Grammy Awards and Billboard Music Awards. In 1996, Public School 155 in New York City was renamed The Jose Feliciano Performing Arts School.

Feliciano is famous not only because of the wonderful songs he writes and sings, but also because he is considered by many to be the first cross-over Puerto Rican artist to have hits in the American pop music scene. He opened the doors for many who have followed, including Jennifer Lopez and Marc Anthony. Lopez, a popular singer and actress, was born in the Bronx, New York, to Puerto Rican parents. She got her big break in show business as a dancer. She took singing and dancing lessons from childhood and has achieved popularity with both Spanish-speaking and English-speaking audiences. She lists Rita Moreno as her biggest inspiration.

Her husband, Puerto Rican recording artist Marc Anthony, is the biggest-selling salsa artist of all time. He has won two Grammy awards and three Latin Grammy awards and has tried his hand at acting as well.

José Feliciano

Many Latin American countries celebrate Carnival with festivals, parades, and parties. Many people dress in colorful costumes, and some even wear masks.

Holidays and Festivals

Holidays and festivals celebrated in Puerto Rico are usually rooted in the country's strong Catholic faith. For example, the Christmas holiday season is celebrated from the day after Thanksgiving until January 6, commonly known as Three Kings' Day. Many of the traditions, including Christmas lights and Santa Claus, are very similar to those practiced in the rest of the United States. People go to church on Christmas Eve, December 24, which is normally a solemn day.

Children who have behaved all year long get toys from Santa Claus on Christmas Day, but that is not the only chance for a holiday gift. It is a tradition to fill a box with straw or grass and place it under the bed on the night of January 5. That night, the Three Kings, or Wise Men, leave presents in exchange for the hay or grass, which they feed to their camels. The tradition is done in remembrance of the kings who brought presents to the newborn Jesus.

After the Three Kings' Festival, the San Sebastian Festival is held in San Juan. It is a gigantic block party where many vendors come to showcase their arts and crafts. Barely a few days go by in Puerto Rico before there is another festival. Just about every town on the island holds a big celebration in honor of its patron saint. The festivals involve food, music, dancing, fireworks, parades, and all types of games and activities for the children.

Mardi Gras, or Carnival, started in the 1700s with closely related celebrations in Brazil and New Orleans. It takes place before Ash Wednesday as Catholics prepare for the Lenten season. Thousands of

About 2 million people attend the Puerto Rican Day Parade on Fifth Avenue in New York City each year. It is held on the second Sunday in June in support of Puerto Ricans everywhere.

people participate in the good time by dressing up in wildly colored costumes and wearing masks of demons. There is nonstop thumping music throughout the event, which ends with a fake funeral for a sardine.

For something less wild, try the Casals Festival. It usually marks the beginning of summer with the premier classical music event in the Caribbean. Pablo Casals was a well-loved Spanish cellist who moved to the island in the 1950s and helped found the Puerto Rico Symphony Orchestra.

While American girls look forward to their Sweet 16 parties, in Puerto Rico the tradition is celebrated a year sooner with a quinceañera. After a religious ceremony, the girl of honor symbolically crosses from girlhood to maturity. One tradition is called the Changing of the Shoes. The girl's father changes her shoes from flats to high heels, signifying her transformation to adulthood. A reception with food, gifts, and dancing follows.

There is even a festival for outdoorsmen. The San Juan International Billfish Tournament is held every year at the end of August into September. It attracts deep-sea fishermen from all over the world. The weeklong event features many prizes and parties as anglers try to catch the biggest marlin and sailfish they can.

People celebrate Three Kings' Day, a major holiday in Puerto Rico where people remember the Wise Men who visited Jesus after his birth.

A centuries-old cannon stands guard at El Morro. In 1595, Sir Francis Drake of England attacked El Morro but failed to take San Juan.

We Visit
Old San Juan

Many visitors will tell you that the most amazing thing about their visit to Puerto Rico was walking through the quaint, narrow streets of Old San Juan. Exploring this area of the city is like walking back through time.

Old San Juan is actually on a small island connected to the main city of San Juan by three bridges. The cobblestone streets and coquina walls from early Spanish settlement remain intact. Guarding the island is the magnificent Fort San Felipe del Morro, the centerpiece of Old San Juan. Known as El Morro, this giant fort was built to protect the town from invaders using San Juan Bay. It was named after the King of Spain when it was built in the sixteenth century. It took forty-eight years to put the walls up around the city. They are twenty feet (six meters) thick.

The 700-acre fort is now a national park and tremendous tourist attraction. On display are cannonballs and guard towers, as well as places where the Spaniards kept prisoners. Visitors are permitted to touch parts of the walls that were damaged by cannonballs fired from attacking ships.

Construction of the six-level fort began in 1540 and took almost fifty years to complete. The fort rises 140 feet above the sea, giving the Spanish soldiers stationed there a chance to spot enemy ships before they got too close.

Visitors take photos sitting atop some of the vintage cannons still in place, then explore the tunnels, dungeons, and guard towers. Many of them notice something strange: People must have been smaller back then, because everything seems so cramped.

There are also several smaller forts, such as San Cristóbal and San Gerónimo, that are also worth visiting. They have moats and tunnels that made them almost impossible to capture. Numerous historic homes and cemeteries in Old San Juan also allow visitors. And of course there are many historic churches to visit, including St. John the Baptist Cathedral, which was built of wood in 1521. Destroyed by a hurricane in 1526, the magnificent cathedral was reconstructed about 20 years later using large stones taken from the mountains near the center of the island. The tomb of Juan Ponce de León is inside the cathedral.

There's also a huge bronze statue of Ponce de León in Plaza de San José (or St. Joseph's Plaza). What's remarkable about the statue is that it was made from cannon captured from the British when they attacked the island in 1797. In the plaza, you can also enjoy a cool drink and mingle with the locals and tourists alike.

For another historical photo opportunity, walk down to the Plaza de Armas (Arms Square). This is the main square of Old San Juan. The plaza features four statues that represent the four seasons. Each statue is more than 100 years old.

Las garitas or sentry boxes were built around the walls of El Morro to help the Spanish see oncoming ships.

Plaza de Armas

Finally let's take a look at a more modern plaza by going to the Plaza del Quinto Centenario (Quincentennial Square). This little park was built in 1992 to celebrate the 500th anniversary of Columbus discovering Puerto Rico.

After all that walking you may want to take a short rest by sitting on of the benches at Parque de las Palomas, which means "Pigeon Park." Feed the birds that gather there and take in the incredible view. From this spot you can see the harbor, the city, and the mountains.

After spending so much time outdoors, you may be ready for some indoor sightseeing. There are more than ten museums in Old San Juan, as well as art galleries. Most of them are inexpensive to enter.

Finished sightseeing? Grab a tropical treat like a *piragua* from a street vendor, then head to the beach to cool off. Don't forget to tell your friends what a great time you had visiting Old San Juan.

Besitos de Coco (Coconut Kisses)

Kids in Puerto Rico love these tasty candies.

Ingredients
2 cups grated coconut or coconut flakes
1 cup water
1½ cups brown sugar
¼ teaspoon vanilla

Directions
1. Put the water and coconut in a pan. Have **an adult** bring the water to a boil.
2. Once it is boiling rapidly, add the brown sugar. Put on oven mitts and stir.
3. Lower the heat on the stove and let the mixture cook for about 30 minutes. Don't forget to stir the mixture occasionally.
4. Once the mixture looks like it is beginning to get hard and sticky, add the vanilla. Stir it again and cook it for just another few minutes. The mixture should get very sticky now.
5. Take one tablespoon of mixture out at a time and drop it on a greased cookie sheet. Let the candy cool, and enjoy your tasty treat!

Carnival Mask

You'll Need:
Aluminum foil
Newspaper
Papier-mâche paste   *This project takes a few days to finish. It is
Paint   important to let the glue completely dry before
Paintbrush   painting your mask.*

1. Cover your work surface with an old tablecloth or shower
   curtain.
2. Tear off a large piece of aluminum foil at least twice as long as
   your face and fold it in half. Gently place the foil over your face
   to create a mold.
3. Crumple up some pieces of newspaper and gently place the
   pieces inside the curved sections of the foil where your face was.
   Now gently place the mold on your work surface.
4. Cover the foil with strips of newspaper soaked in papier-mâche
   paste. Be careful not to press down too hard on the foil. Apply
   four or five layers of the glue-soaked newspaper strips, making
   sure they are dry before you apply the next layer.
5. When everything is dry, repeat the papier-mâche process to
   create and attach horns or large ears to make your mask scary.
6. After the mask has dried, cut out the eyes and the mouth with
   scissors.
7. Once everything is totally dry (this may take a few days)
   decorate your mask with colorful paint. Add horns, giant ears, or
   anything else to make your mask look funny and maybe a little
   scary!

1493 Columbus discovers Puerto Rico on his second voyage to the New World.

1508 The Spaniards begin colonizing the island.

1509 Juan Ponce de León is named governor of the island.

1513 African slaves are brought to the island.

1514 Spanish settlers begin to marry Taíno Indian women.

1522 San José Church is established.

1523 The first sugarcane processing plant is built.

1539 Construction begins on a giant fort, El Morro.

1595 Sir Francis Drake of England attacks San Juan; the guns at El Morro repel his fleet.

1634 More forts are built to protect San Juan harbor.

1702 The British attack the island but are turned away.

1835 Spain abolishes slavery in its colonies.

1843 A lighthouse is built atop El Morro.

1849 The book *El Jibaro* is published.

1868 Several hundred people revolt for independence.

1898 The U.S. defeats Spain in the Spanish-American War and takes control of Puerto Rico.

1917 The Jones-Shafroth Act is signed, giving Puerto Ricans U.S. citizenship.

1945 Puerto Ricans start moving to the United States mainland looking for better jobs.

1948 Luis Muñoz Marín is elected governor of Puerto Rico; he takes office January 2, 1949.

1950 Puerto Rico is able to draft its own constitution.

1961 Actress Rita Moreno wins an Academy Award.

1973 Roberto Clemente is inducted to the Baseball Hall of Fame.

1993 English and Spanish are declared the official languages of Puerto Rico.

2006 A special sales tax is set up to help offset cash shortages in government.

2009 Thousands of workers march in San Juan to protest possible job layoffs. An entire neighborhood in San Juan is evacuated due to a major fire that started because of an explosion at a nearby oil refinery. The explosion's strength is equivalent to a 2.8 magnitude earthquake.

2010 In an effort to lure a Major League Baseball team to represent Puerto Rico, San Juan hosts a three-game series between the Florida Marlins and the New York Mets.

Books

Bernier-Grand, Carmen T. *Shake It Morena and Other Folklore from Puerto Rico.* Millbrook Press, 2006.

Brown, Jonathan. *Puerto Rico and Other Outlying Areas.* New York: Gareth Stevens Publishing, 2005.

Foley, Erin. *Puerto Rico.* Tarrytown, NY: Benchmark Books, 2010.

Gutner, Howard. *Puerto Rico.* Danbury, CT: Children's Press 2009.

Zapata, Elizabeth. *Puerto Rico.* Danbury, CT: Children's Press 2007.

Works Consulted

Acosta-Belen, Edna, and Carlos Santiago. *Puerto Ricans in the United States.* Boulder, CO: Lynne Reinner Publishers, 2006.

Ayala, Cesar, and Rafael Bernabe. *Puerto Rico in the American Century: A History Since 1898.* Chapel Hill: University of North Carolina Press, 2009.

Bernier-Grand, Carmen T. *Poet and Politician of Puerto Rico: Don Luis Muñoz Marín.* New York: Orchand Books, 1995.

Deland, Jack. *Puerto Rico Mio.* Washington, DC: Smithsonian Press, 1990.

Muckley, Robert, and Adela Martinez-Santiago. *Stories from Puerto Rico.* New York: McGraw Hill Publishing, 1999.

Marino, John. *Frommer's Puerto Rico, 9th Edition.* New York: Wiley Publishing, 2009.

Rouse, Irving. *The Taínos.* New Haven, CT: Yale University Press, 1993.

Van Middeldyk, R.A. *History of Puerto Rico: From the Spanish Discovery to the American Occupation.* Manchester, NH: Ayer Company Publishers, 1975; reprinted Charleston, SC: Biblio Bazaar, 2006.

On the Internet

El Boricua
http://www.elboricua.com

Frommer's Puerto Rico
http://www.frommers.com/destinations/puertorico/

The Islands of Puerto Rico
http://www.gotopuertorico.com

Meet Puerto Rico
http://www.meetpuertorico.com

Puerto Rico Vacations
http://www.caribbeantravel.com/puertorico

Welcome to Puerto Rico
http://www.topuertorico.org

archipelago (ar-kih-PEH-leh-goh)—A chain of islands.

boricua (buh-REE-kwah)—The Taíno term for someone who was born and raised in Puerto Rico.

Carnival (KAR-nuh-val)—The festive season just before the solemn Catholic holiday of Lent.

commonwealth (KAH-mun-welth)—A self-governing territory that is part of the United States; an area that is governed by its people.

cosmopolitan (koz-moh-PAH-lih-tin)—Having to do with a city; belonging to the world.

karst—A region with sinkholes, underground streams, and caverns.

patron saint (PAY-trun SAYNT)—A designated saint who protects and helps a church, city, nation, or other area.

quinceañera (keen-say-ah-NYAYR-ah)—A coming-out party for a girl on her fifteenth birthday.

salsa (SOL-suh)—Latin American dance music and the lively, spicy dance performed to it.

stalactite (stuh-LAK-tyt)—A formation of calcium carbonate that resembles an icicle hanging from the roof of a cave.

stalagmite (stuh-LAG-myt)—A formation of calcium carbonate that grows upward from the floor of a cave as water containing the mineral calcite accumulates.

Salsa dancing

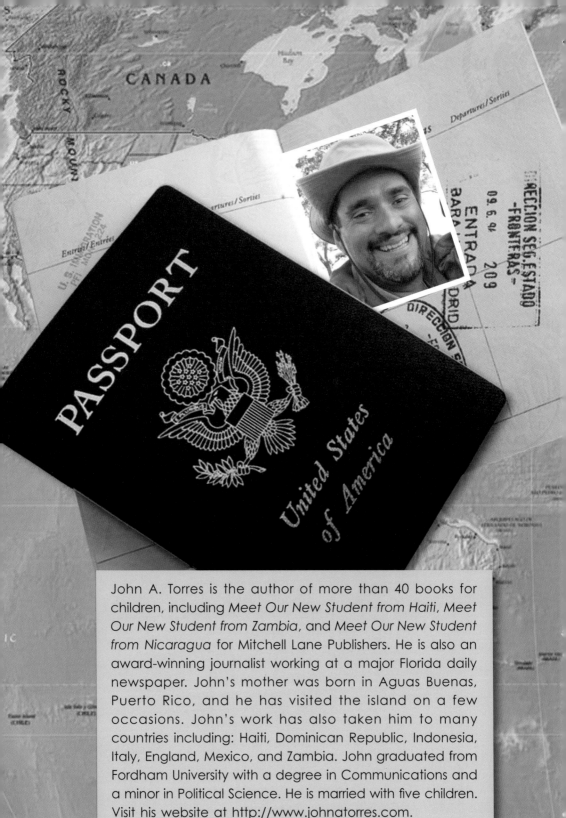

John A. Torres is the author of more than 40 books for children, including *Meet Our New Student from Haiti*, *Meet Our New Student from Zambia*, and *Meet Our New Student from Nicaragua* for Mitchell Lane Publishers. He is also an award-winning journalist working at a major Florida daily newspaper. John's mother was born in Aguas Buenas, Puerto Rico, and he has visited the island on a few occasions. John's work has also taken him to many countries including: Haiti, Dominican Republic, Indonesia, Italy, England, Mexico, and Zambia. John graduated from Fordham University with a degree in Communications and a minor in Political Science. He is married with five children. Visit his website at http://www.johnatorres.com.